Piano • Vocal • Guitar

Best of
CURTIS MAYFIELD

Cover photo © Everett Collection Inc / Alamy

ISBN 978-1-4803-3246-1

HAL•LEONARD®
CORPORATION

7777 W. BLUEMOUND RD. P.O. BOX 13819 MILWAUKEE, WI 53213

In Australia Contact:
Hal Leonard Australia Pty. Ltd.
4 Lentara Court
Cheltenham, Victoria, 3192 Australia
Email: ausadmin@halleonard.com.au

Visit Hal Leonard Online at
www.halleonard.com

Best of Curtis Mayfield

FREDDIE'S DEAD

Words and Music by
CURTIS MAYFIELD

sure all would a-gree that his mis-er-y___ was his wom-an and

Emaj7

things. Now Fred-die's dead, that's what I said. ___

F#m7

Ev-'ry-bod - y's mis-used him,

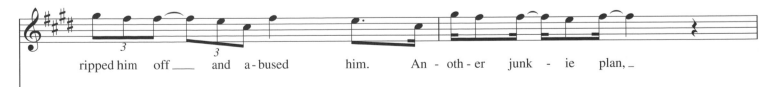

ripped him off ___ and a-bused him. An-oth-er junk-ie plan, _

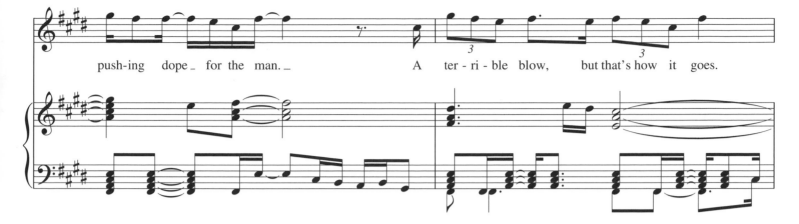

push-ing dope _ for the man. _ A ter-ri-ble blow, but that's how it goes.

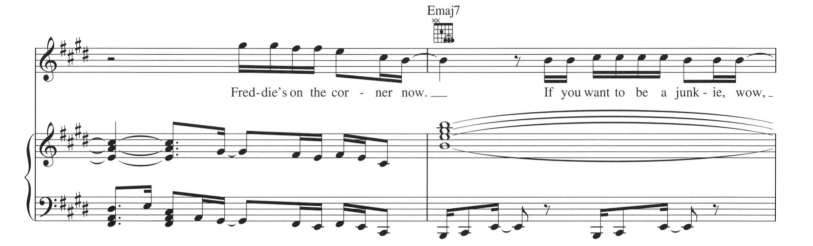

Emaj7

Fred-die's on the cor - ner now. _ If you want to be a junk - ie, wow, _

_ re-mem-ber Fred-die's dead. _

F♯m7

We're all ___ built up ___ with prog - ress. _ But

some - times I must con - fess, we can deal with rock - ets and dreams, but re -

al - i - ty, what does it mean? Ain't noth - in' said,

Emaj7

'cause Fred - die's dead. Hey,

hey. Lord, Lord,

hey, ___ hey, ___ yeah, _

___ yeah, ___ uh, ___ huh, ___

Lord, ___ Lord, ___ yeah, _

___ yeah, ___ huh, ___ huh, ___

yeah, ___ yeah, ___ Fred-die's dead. ___

Play 4 times

N.C.

F#m7

All I want is some peace of mind ___ with a lit-tle love ___ I'm try-in' to find. ___ This could

be such a beau-ti-ful world, ___ with a won-der-ful girl, ___ oo. ___ I need a wom-an, child. ___

Don't wan - na be like Fred-die, now ___ 'cause Fred-die's dead. _

Hey, ___ hey, ___

yeah, ___ yeah. ___ If you don't try _

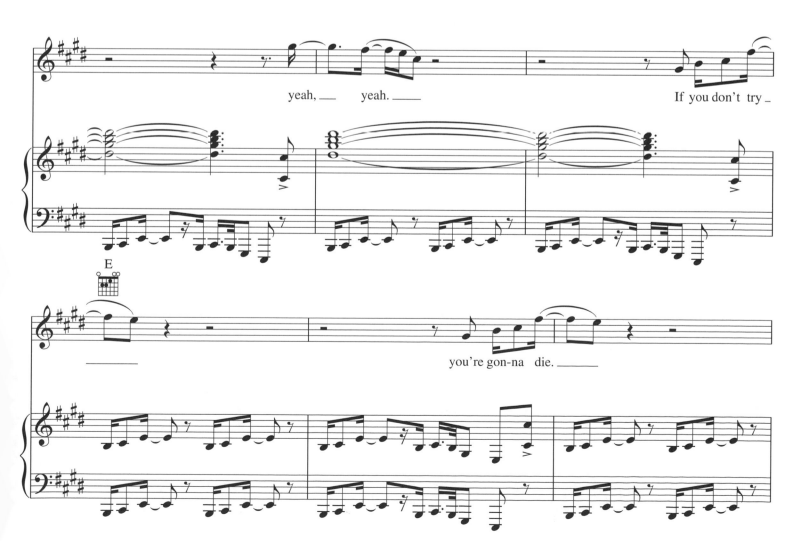

you're gon-na die. ___

F#m7

Why can't we broth-ers pro-tect one an-oth-er? No one's se-ri-ous and it makes me fu-ri-ous.

Emaj7

Don't be mis-led, just think of Fred.

Emaj7

Ev-

F#m7

-'ry-bod-y's mis-used him,_ ripped_ him off_ and a-bused him._ An-

oth-er junk-ie plan,_ push-ing dope_ for the man._

Emaj7

Fred-dies's on the cor-ner now. If you

wan-na be a junk-ie, wow,_ re-mem-ber Fred-die's dead._

14

Huh, ___ huh, _ huh, _ huh, _ huh, _

Fred-die's dead, ___ hey, _

___ hey, _____ huh, _
___ Lord, _____ huh, _

Repeat and Fade

___ huh. _____ Lord, _
___ huh. _____ Hey, _

GET DOWN

Words and Music by
CURTIS MAYFIELD

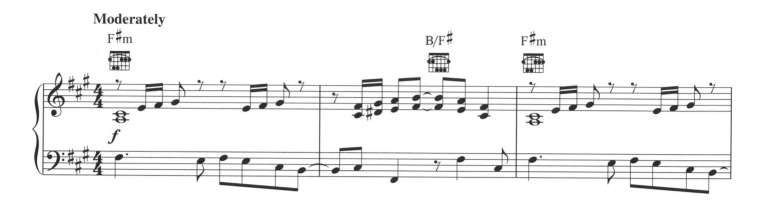

Get down,
baby,
baby,

to the funk - y, funk - y, funk - y groove. ___ Get down,
as the rhy - thms shoot fire ___ through your a - ble soul. ___ Get down,

baby, let the light re-flect up-on your
baby, play the part like a pro in a

nat-'ral mood. Get down, baby, your cre-
per-fect role. Get down, baby, to the

a-tive mood___ shall ex-press it-self. Get down, ba - by,
funk-y, funk - y, funk-y groove. Get down, ba - by,

af-ter life and de-sire there is noth-ing left. We're all
let the light re-flect up - on your nat-'ral mood. One can

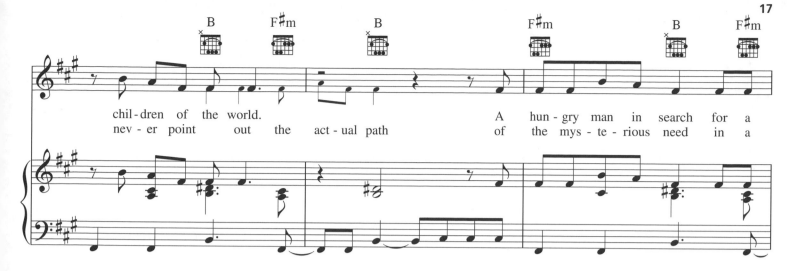

chil-dren of the world.
A hun-gry man in search for a
nev-er point out the act-ual path
of the mys-te-rious need in a

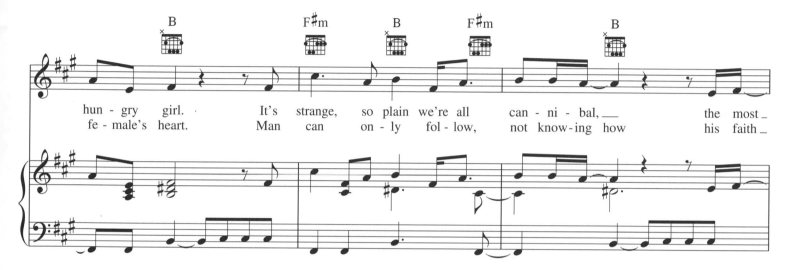

hun-gry girl. It's strange, so plain we're all can-ni-bal, the most
fe-male's heart. Man can on-ly fol-low, not know-ing how his faith

wast-ed and two-faced of all an-i-mal. Get down,
might e-rupt in his hun-gry prowl.

get down, get down,

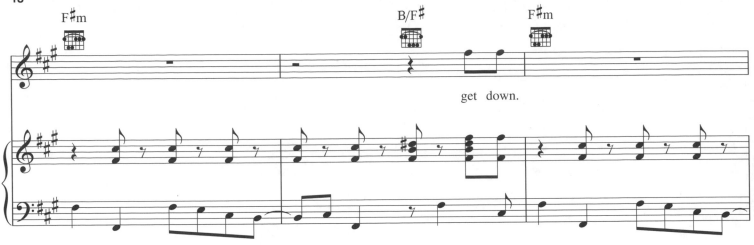

get down.

Take my soul, ba - by, when you're
Get down.

real, I can feel so much de - sire. Take my soul, ba - by,

life un - folds __ from my soul __ and it's all a - fire. So get

down.

Just get down.

D. S. al Coda

Get down,

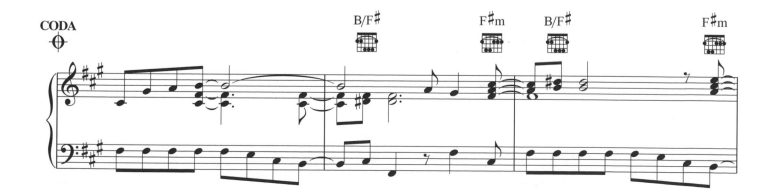

CODA

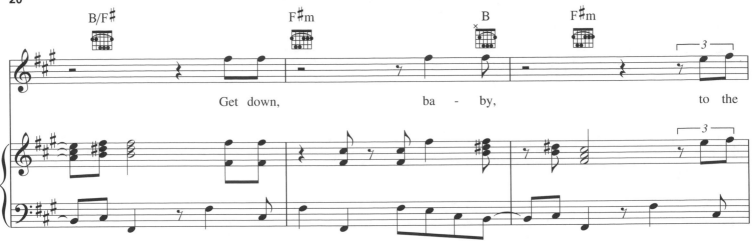

Get down, ba - by, to the

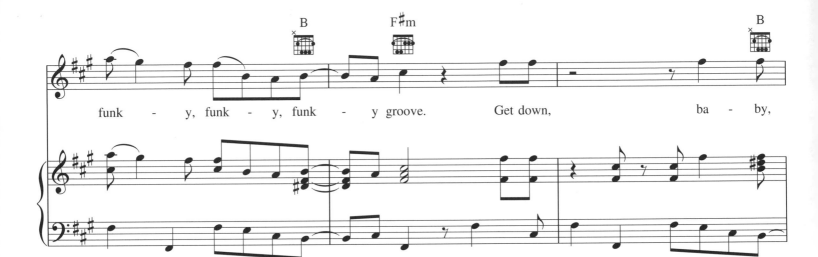

funk - y, funk - y, funk - y groove. Get down, ba - by,

let the light re - flect __ up - on your nat - 'ral mood. Take my soul,

ba - by, your cre - a - tive mood __ shall ex - press

it - self.   Take my soul,   ba - by,   af - ter

life   and   de - sire,   there   is   noth - ing   left.   Get   down,

get   down,

Repeat and Fade

get   down,

Optional Ending

get   down.

GHETTO CHILD
(Little Child Runnin' Wild)

Words and Music by
CURITS MAYFIELD

Moderately

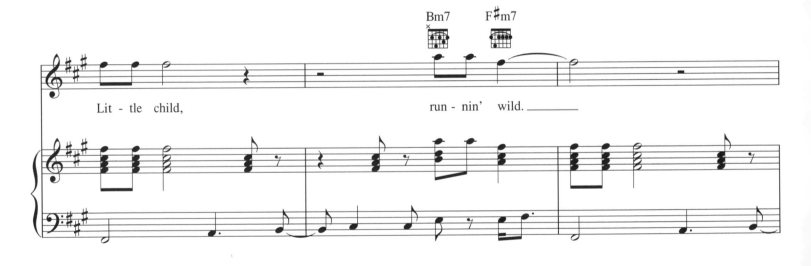

Lit - tle child,   run - nin' wild. _____

Watch a while, _____   you see, he nev - er smiles. _

Bro - ken home,
One room shack

Bm7 F#m7   Bm7

fa - ther gone, _____
on the al - ley back. _____
run - nin' through my bones. _____

ma - ma tired, _____
Con - trol, I'm told, _____
I'm sor - ry, son, _____

F#m7

so he's all a - lone. _____
from a - cross the track. _____
all your mon - ey's gone. _____

Where

Bm7 F#m7

Kind of sad,   kind of mad, _____
is the mayor   who'll make all things fair? _____
Pain - ful rip   in my up - per hip. _____

ghet - to child, _____ think - in' he's been had. __
He lives out - side _____ our pol - lut - ed air. __
I guess it's time _____ to take an - oth - er trip. __

__ In the back of his mind he's say - in', And I did - n't have to
__ Don't care no what no -

be here. You did - n't have to
bo - dy say, I got to take the

love for me, __ while I was just a noth - ing child.
pain a - way. __ It's get - tin' wors - er day by day,

To Coda ⊕

Why could-n't they just   let me be,   let me be,
and all my life just has

F#m7   Bm7   F#m7

let me be,   let me be? ____   *Instrumental solo*

Bm7

F#m7   1

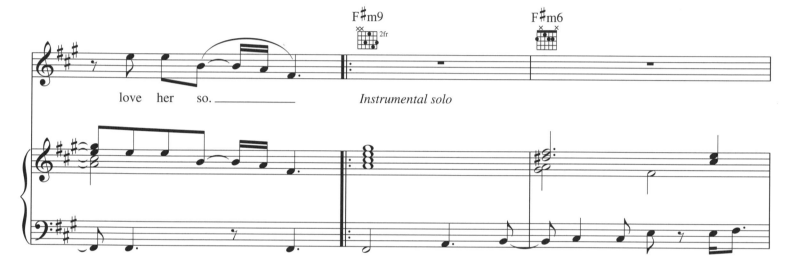

Would rip her, but I love her so,

love her so. _____ *Instrumental solo*

F#m9 F#m6

F#m9 F#m6 Bm9 Bm7

F#m9 F#m6

Optional Ending
F#m9

Repeat and Fade

GYPSY WOMAN

Words and Music by
CURTIS MAYFIELD

car - a - van, __ she was danc - ing with all the men. __

Wait - ing for the ris - ing sun, __ ev - 'ry - one was __

__ hav - in' fun. __ I hate to see the lad - y go, __

C#m7

know - ing she'll __ nev - er know __ that I love her, __

I love her. ___ The

gyp - sy wom - an, _____ A gyp - sy wom - an. _____

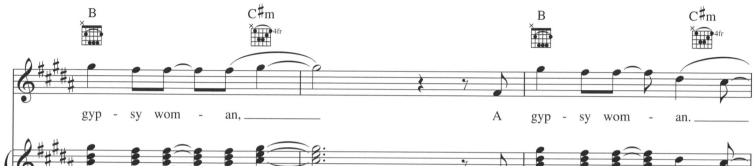

___ A gyp - sy wom - an, _____ a

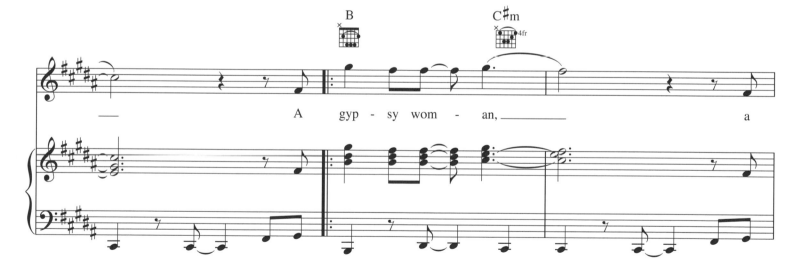

Repeat and Fade **Optional Ending**

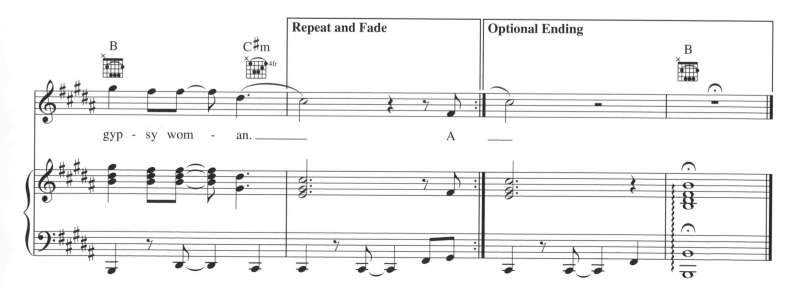

gyp - sy wom - an. _____ A ___

HOOKED ON YOUR LOVE

Words and Music by
CURTIS MAYFIELD

Your ten-der smile ___ gives me ___ hap-py thoughts of you. ___

You've got me so close ___ to my dreams ___ now, they

have to come true. ___ Ooh, ___ ba-by, noth-ing to ___ be ___ shy ___

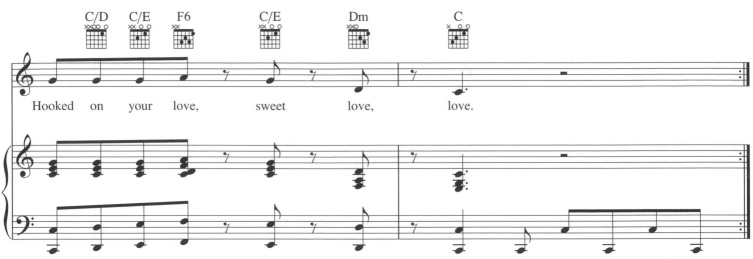

Hooked on your love, sweet love, love.

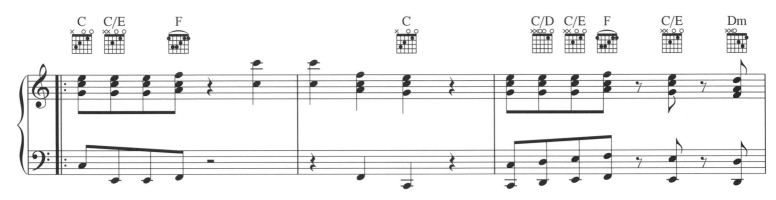

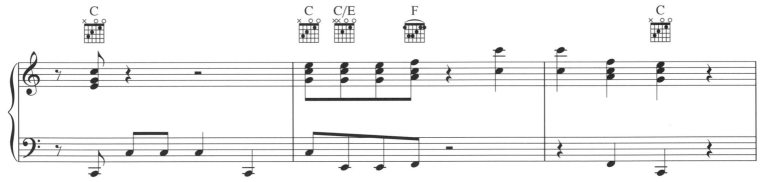

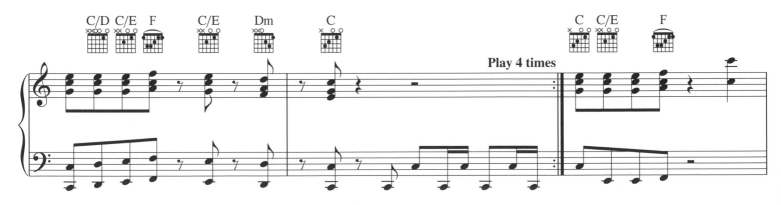

Play 4 times

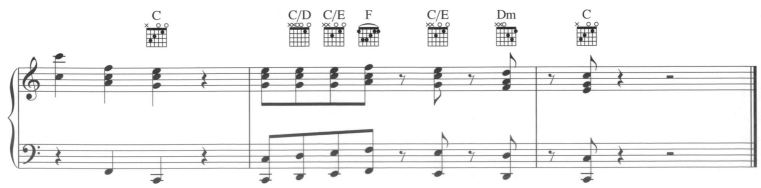

IT'S ALL RIGHT

Words and Music by
CURTIS MAYFIELD

Early R&B Shuffle

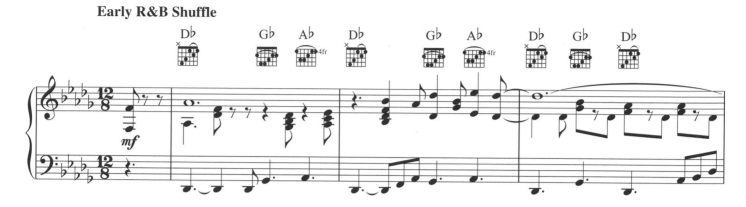

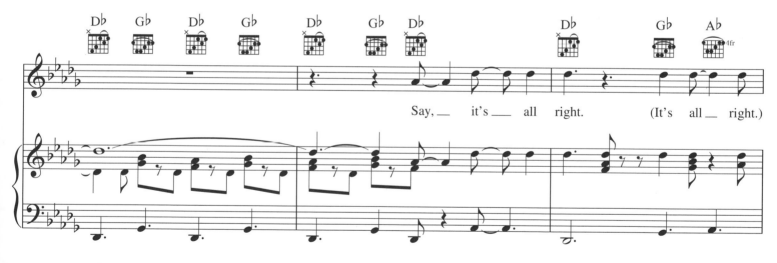

Say, __ it's __ all right. (It's all __ right.)

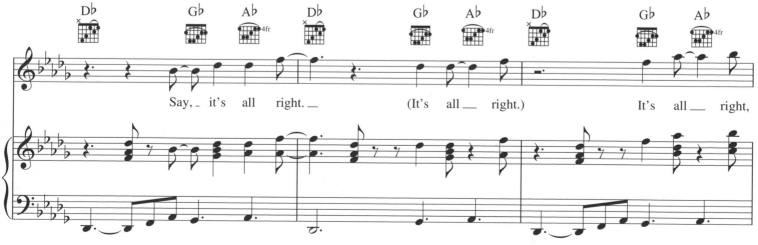

Say, __ it's all right. __ (It's all __ right.) It's all __ right,

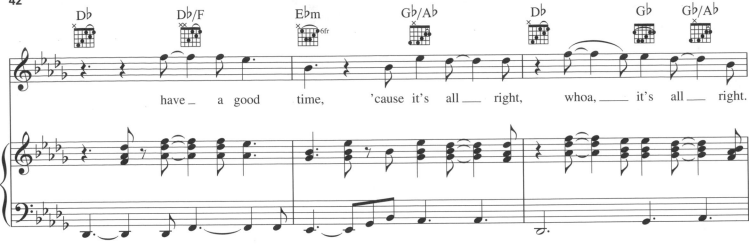

have _ a good time, 'cause it's all _ right, whoa, _ it's all _ right.

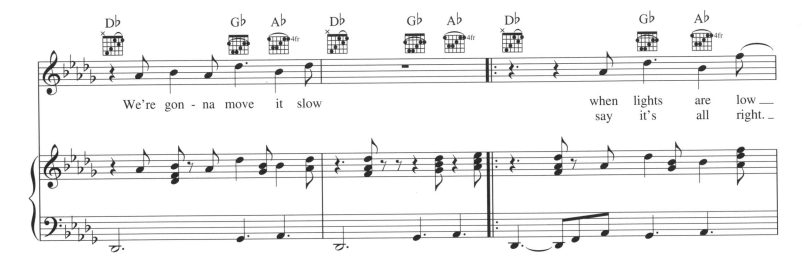

We're gon - na move it slow when lights are low _
say it's all right. _

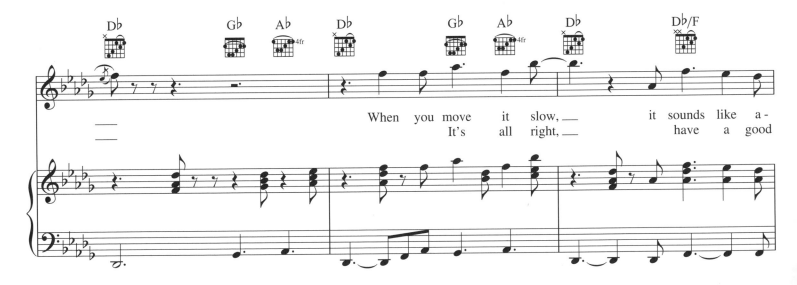

When you move it slow, _ it sounds like a -
It's all right, _ have a good

more, _ and it's all _ right, whoa, _ it's all _ right.
time, _ 'cause it's all _ right, whoa, _ it's all _ right.

Now — lis - ten to the beat,
Now, ev - 'ry - bod - y clap your hands,

kind - a pat your fe - et.
give your - self a chance. ____ You got — soul, —

— and ev - 'ry - bod - y knows — that it's all — right, whoa, — it's all — right.

When you wake up ____ ear - ly in the
Some - day I'll find me a

mor - ning   feel - in' sad __ like __ so man - y of __
wom - an   who will love __ and __ treat me real nice.

__ us do,   hum __ a lit - tle soul,   make
Then my woe's got to go,   and my

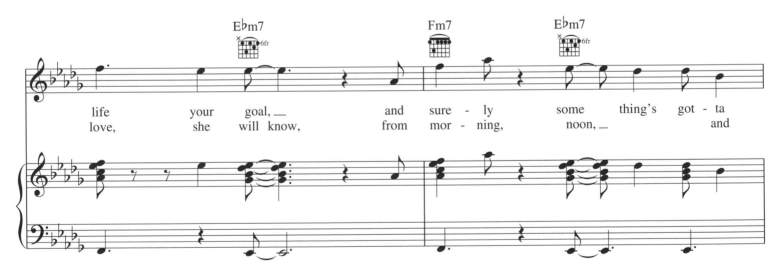

life your goal, __   and sure - ly   some thing's got - ta
love, she will know,   from mor - ning,   noon, __   and

come to you. __   And say it's all _____ right,

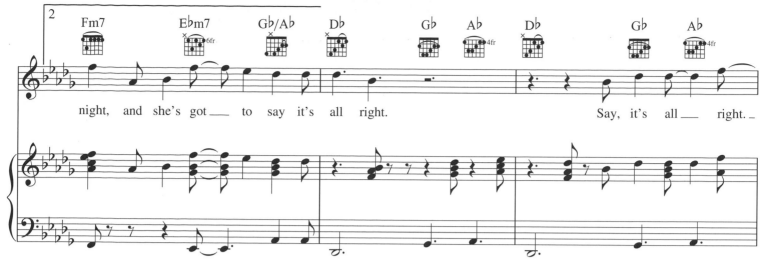

night, and she's got ___ to say it's all right.   Say, it's all ___ right. _

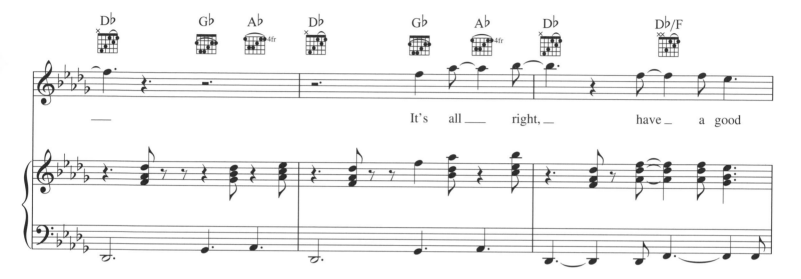

___   It's all ___ right, _   have _ a good

time, _   'cause it's all ___ right,   whoa, ___ it's all ___ right.   *Vocal ad lib to end*

Repeat and Fade | **Optional Ending**

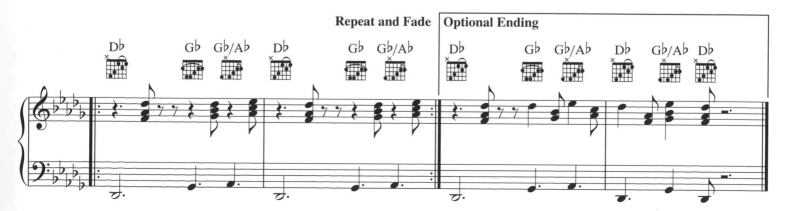

KEEP ON PUSHING

Words and Music by
CURTIS MAYFIELD

now.
see?

Move up   a lit - tle

A great   big

high - er,

stone wall

some   way,   a - some

stands   there   a - head of

how.

me.

'Cause I've   got   my

But I've   got   my

F#m7

C#m7

B

strength,   and it   don't make   sense   not to

pride,   and I'll   move a - long   side   and

keep on ____ push -

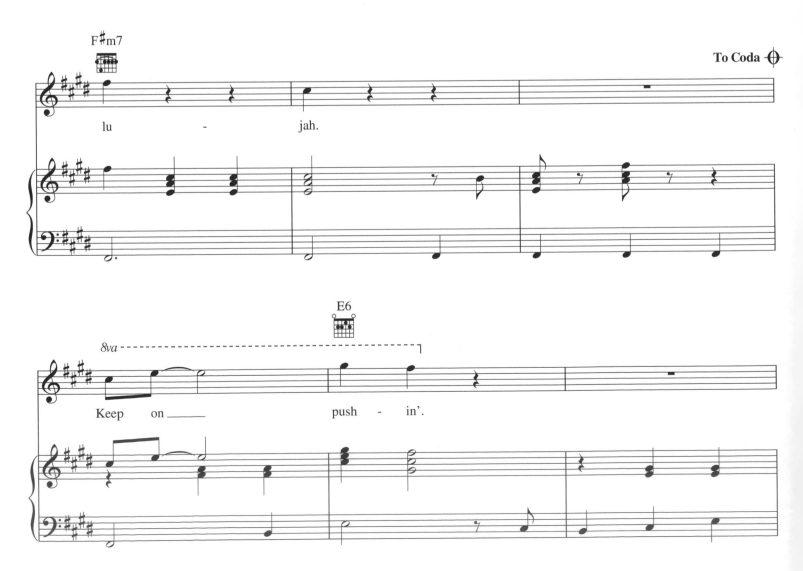

Now may-be some-day (Mmm.) _____

_____ I'll reach that high - er goal.

I know I can make it

with just a lit - tle bit of soul.

'Cause I've got my strength, and it don't make

sense not to keep on _____ push - in'.

D.S. al Coda

Now look - a - look, (Look - a - look.) a - look - a

CODA

Keep on _____ push - in'.

KUNG FU

Words and Music by
CURTIS MAYFIELD

Relaxed R&B Groove

Our days of com-fort, days of night,

don't put your-self in sol - i - tude.

Who can I trust with my

life, when peo - ple tend to be so rude?

My ma - ma bore me in a ghet - to,
sis - ters. My broth - er worked for Un - cle

there was no mat - tress for my

head. But no, she could-n't call me Je - sus.
Sam. It's just a shame, ain't it, mis - ter,

I was - n't white e - nough, she said.
we be - ing broth - ers of the damned?

And then she named me, y'all, Kung Fu. Don't have to ex - plain __ it, no,
Keep your head high, Kung Kung Fu. I will 'til I die, __ yeah,

Kung Fu. Don't know how you'll take it, yeah, Kung Fu. I'm
Kung Fu. Don't be too in - tense, no, Kung Fu. Keep

just tryin' to make __ it, yeah, Kung Fu.
your com - mon sense, __ yeah, Kung Fu.

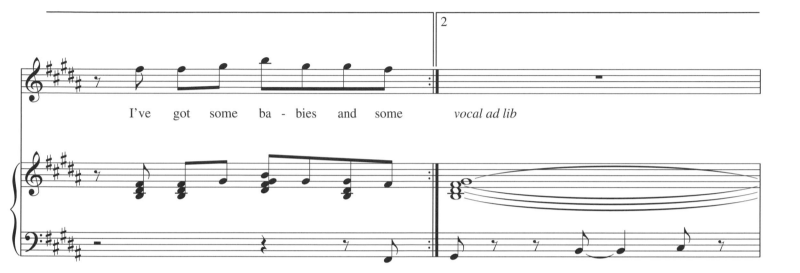

I've got some ba - bies and some *vocal ad lib*

Don't you mis - take life for a

1. sec - ret,   there is no se - cret part of you.
2. *Instrumental break (drums only)*
3. ghet - to.   There was no mat - tress for my head.

You bet your life if you think wick - ed,
But no, she could - n't name me Jes - us.

some - one is think - ing wick - ed too. __
I was - n't white e - nough, she said. __

My ma - ma bore me in a

And then she named＿ me, y'all, Kung Fu. Don't have to ex-plain＿ it, no,

Kung Fu. Don't know how you'll take＿ it, yeah, Kung Fu. I'm

just tryin' to make＿ it, yeah, Kung Fu. Huh,

Kung Fu. Yeah, Kung Fu.

THE MAKINGS OF YOU

Words and Music by
CURTIS MAYFIELD

Bright Waltz, with a lilt

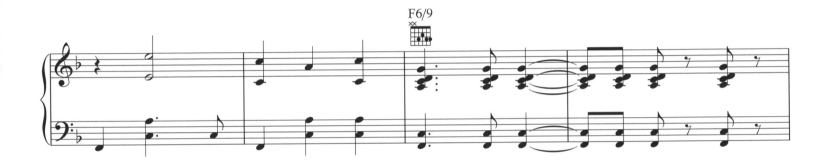

Laid-Back Soul Groove

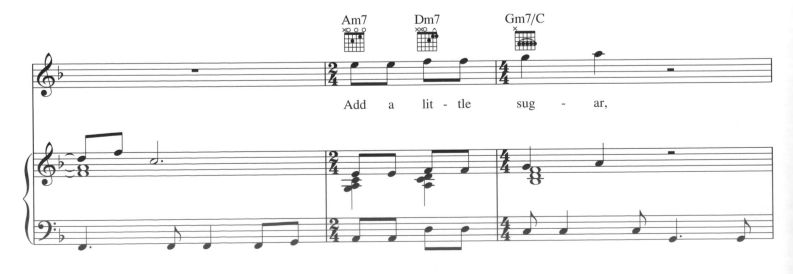

Add a lit-tle sug - ar,

-ings _ of you, _ it is true, _____ the mak - ings _ of

you. _____ The right - eous way to

go, lit - tle one _ would know. _ or be - lieve if I told _ them so _

_____ You're sec - ond _____ to none. _____ The

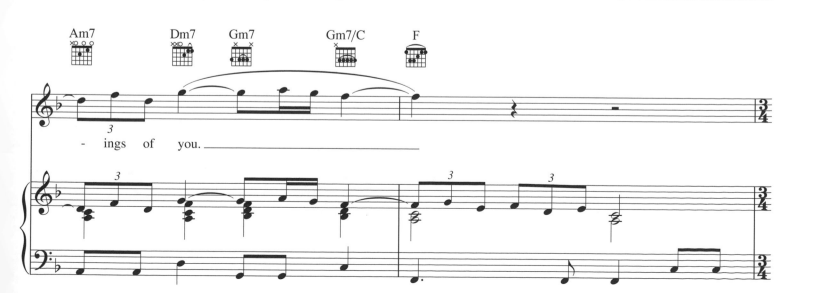

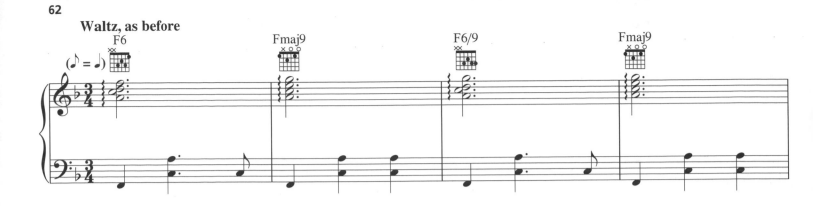

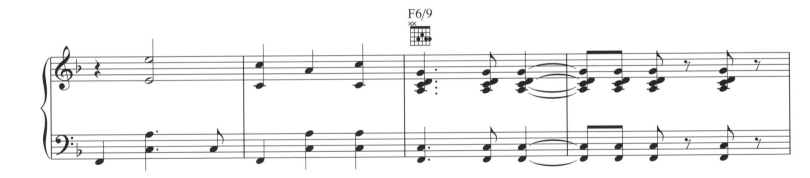

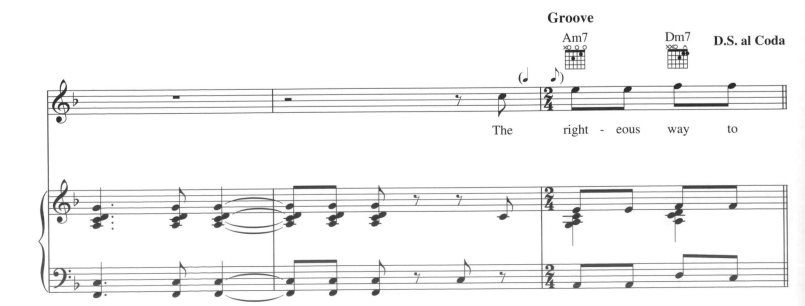

The right - eous way to

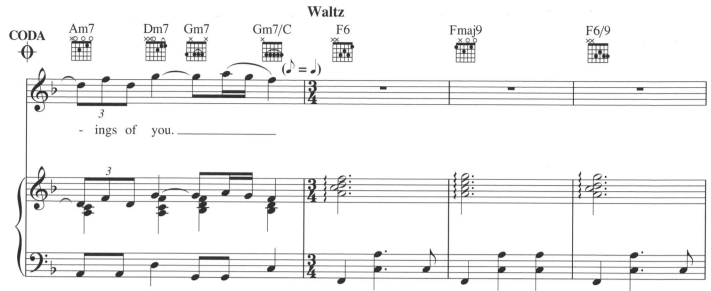

-ings of you. _____

Repeat and Fade **Optional Ending**

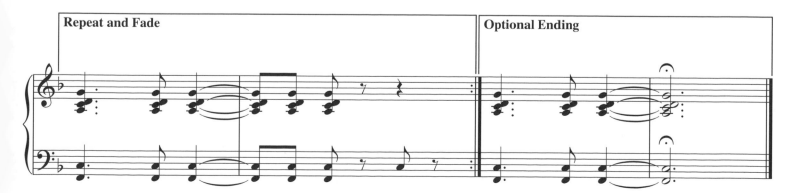

MOVE ON UP

Words and Music by
CURTIS MAYFIELD

Moderately Fast

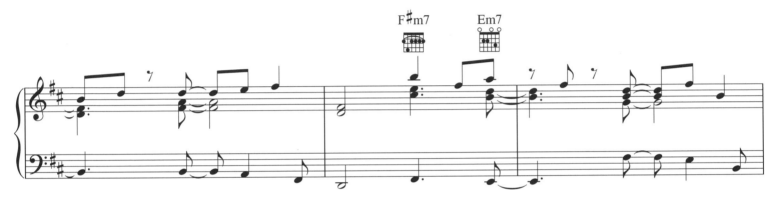

Hush _ now, child, _

and don't you cry. _____

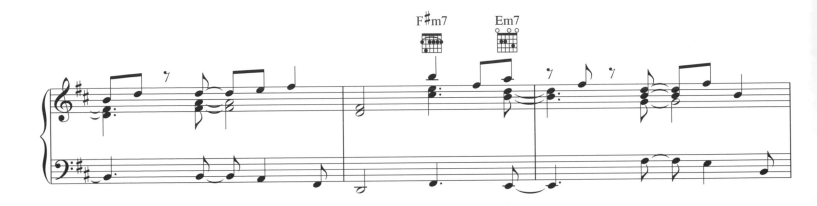

Bite your lip,
Take noth - ing less

and take a trip,
than the su - preme best.

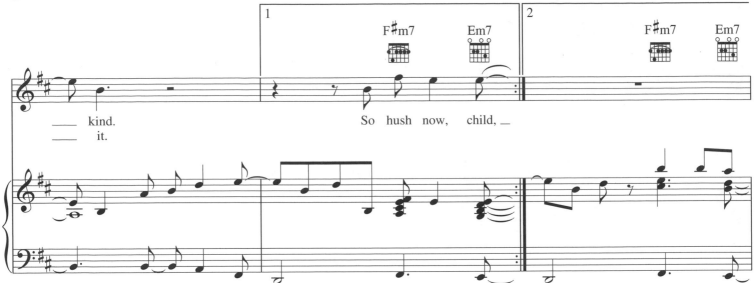

kind.
it.

So hush now, child, __

Just move on up,

move on up.   But move on up,

oh child, ___ but just a-move on up.

But move on up,   move on up.

Repeat and Fade

Optional Ending

PEOPLE GET READY

Words and Music by
CURTIS MAYFIELD

(1., D.S.) Peo-ple, get read - y. There's a train a-com - ing. You don't need no bag - gage, you just

(2.) Peo-ple, get read - y. There's a train to Jor - dan, pick - ing up pas - sen-gers from

get on board. _ All you need is faith _ to hear the die - sels hum - ming.

coast to coast. _ Faith is key, _ o - pen the doors and board _ them.

Don't need no tick - et, you just thank the Lord. _

There's hope for all _ a-mong the loved the most. _

CODA

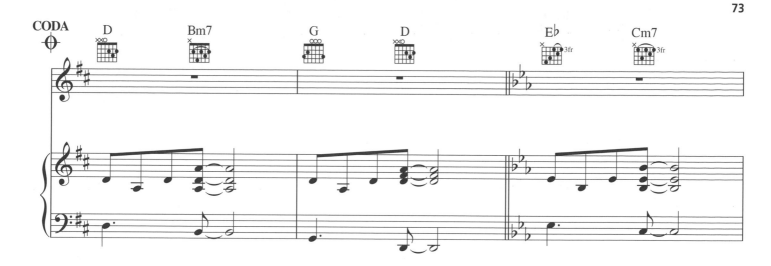

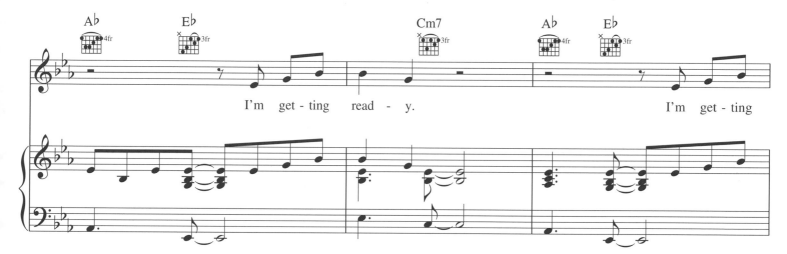

I'm get-ting read - y.   I'm get-ting

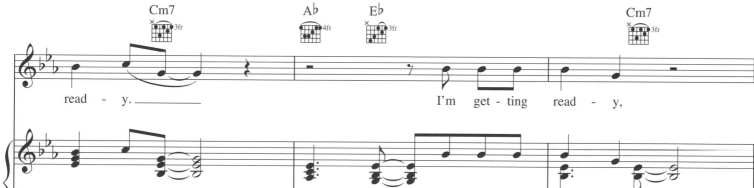

read - y. _____   I'm get-ting read - y,

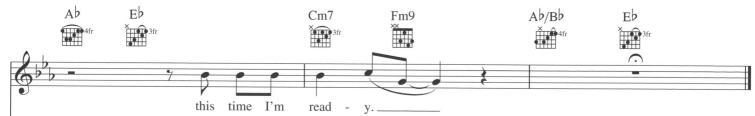

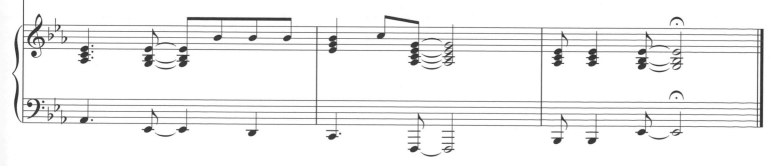

this time I'm read - y. _____

SOMETHING HE CAN FEEL

Words and Music by
CURTIS MAYFIELD

Moderately slow

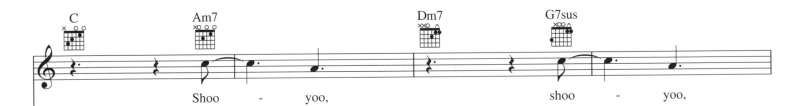

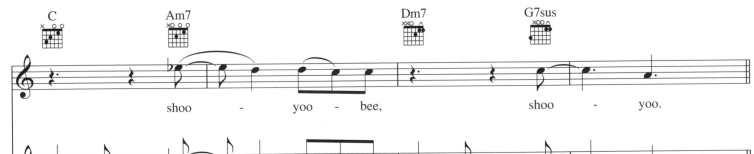

*Recorded a half step lower.

SUPERFLY

Words and Music by
CURTIS MAYFIELD

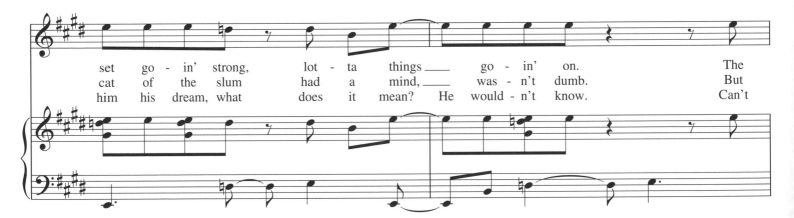

ah, ah. The game he plays, he plays ___ for keeps.

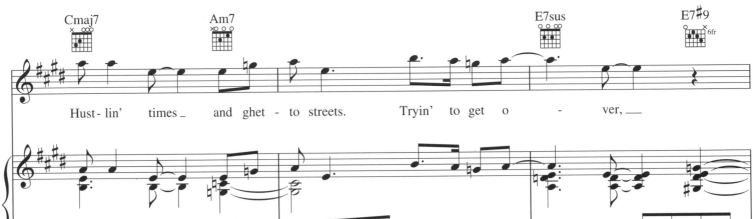

Hust - lin' times __ and ghet - to streets. Tryin' to get o - ver, __

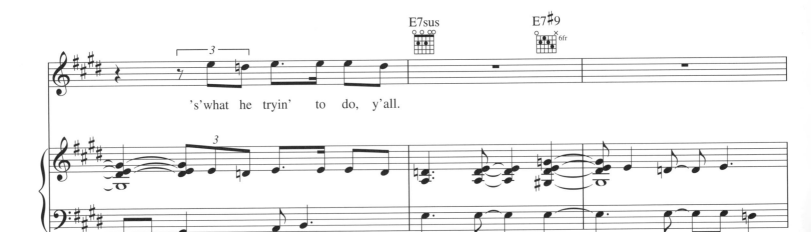

's'what he tryin' to do, y'all.

Tak - in' all __ that he __ can take, gam - blin' with __ the odds

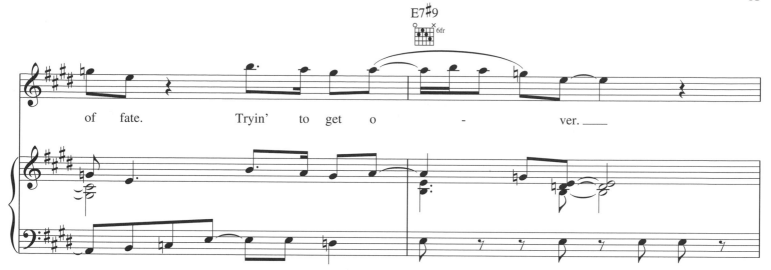

of fate. Tryin' to get o - ver. ___

Tryin' to get o - ver. ___ Tryin' to get o -

- ver. ___ Tryin' to get o - ver. ___

Ooh, su - per - fly.

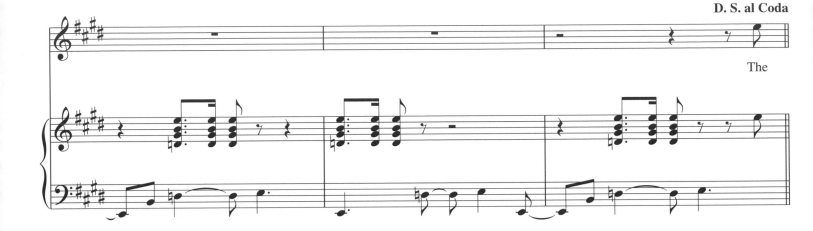

D. S. al Coda

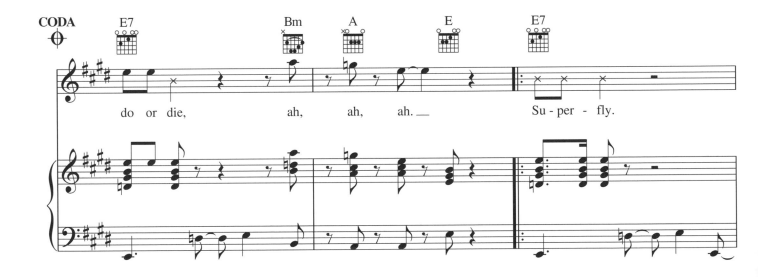

The

CODA

E7   Bm   A   E   E7

do or die,   ah,   ah,   ah. ___   Su - per - fly.

Su - per - fly,   huh,

Tryin' to get o - ver. ___ Tryin' to get o-

- ver. ___ Tryin' to get o - ver. ___

Tryin' to get o - ver. ___ Tryin' to get o-

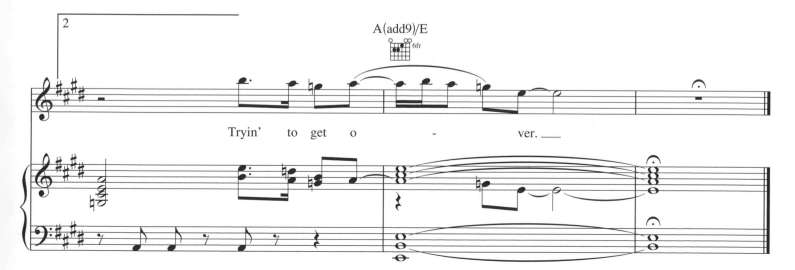

Tryin' to get o - ver. ___

WE'RE A WINNER

Words and Music by
CURTIS MAYFIELD

Moderate Groove, loose 16ths

We're a win-ner, and nev-er let an-y-bod-y say, "Boy,

you can't make it. 'cause a fee-ble mind__ is in your__ way." No more

tears do we cry, __ and we have fi-n'lly dried our eyes. __ And we're

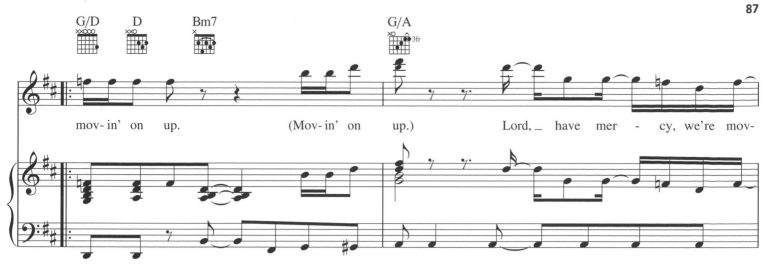

mov-in' on up. (Mov-in' on up.) Lord,__ have mer - cy, we're mov-

- in' on up. (Mov-in' on up.) We're liv-in'
I don't

proof and all's_ a - lert that we're too from the good black dirt.___ And we're a
mind leav-in'__ here, to show the world we have no fear,___ 'cause we're a

win - ner,
win - ner, and ev-'ry-bod-y knows it too.__ We just keep on

PUSHER MAN

Words and Music by
CURTIS MAYFIELD

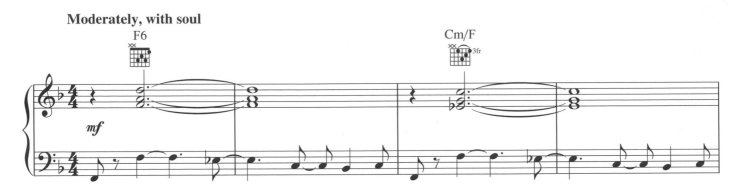

I'm your ma - ma, I'm your dad - dy, I'm that nig - ger in the al - ley.
Ain't I clean? Bad ma - chine, su - per cool, su - per mean.
Heav - y mind have you signed? Mak - in' mon - ey all the time.

ger in the al - ley. I'm your doc - tor when in need, ___ want some coke,
su - per mean. Feel - in' good for the man, su - per - fly,
ey all the time. My L. D. en - trusts me for all junk -

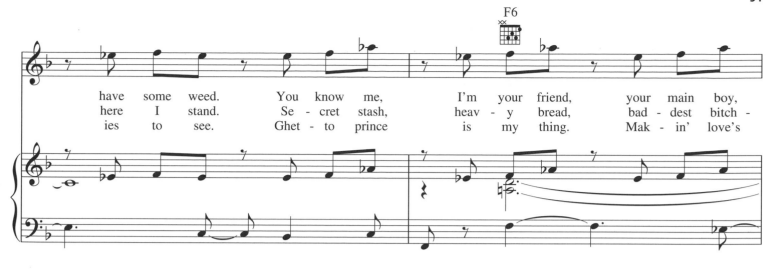

have some weed. You know me, I'm your friend, your main boy,
here I stand. Se - cret stash, heav - y bread, bad - dest bitch -
ies to see. Ghet - to prince is my thing. Mak - in' love's

F6

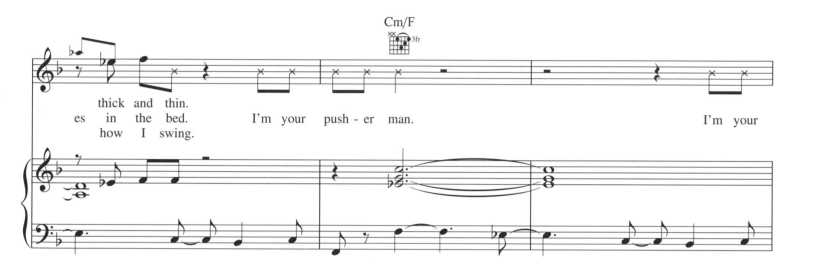

thick and thin.
es in the bed. I'm your push - er man. I'm your
how I swing.

Cm/F

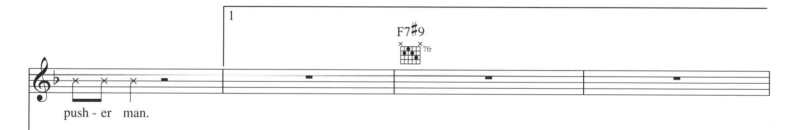

push - er man.

1

F7#9

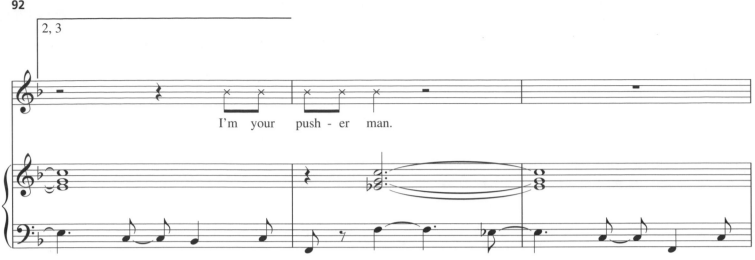

I'm your push - er man.

So - lid life of crime.
Two bags, please. For a gen - er - ous fee,

Make your world what you want it to be.

A man of odd cir - cum - stance,

a vic - tim of ghet - to de - mands.
Got a wom - an I love des - p'rate - ly.

Feed me mon - ey for style, _____
Wan - na give her some - thin' bet - ter than me. ___

and I'll let you trip for a while. _____
Been told I can't be noth - in' else. ___

In - se - cure ___ from the past. ___
Just a hust - ler in spite ___ of my - self. ___ I know ___

How long ___ can a good thing ___ last? ___
___ I can rake ___ it, this life ___ just don't make it.

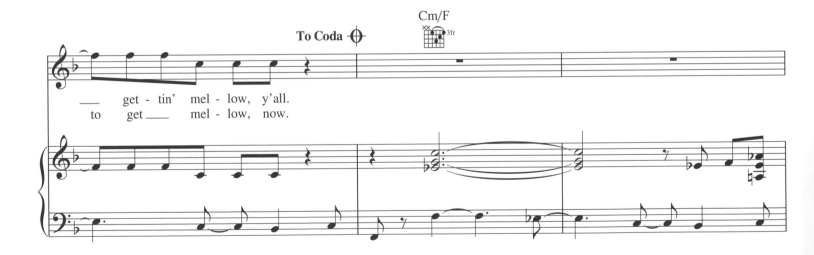

D.C. al Coda

CODA

I'm your ma - ma, I'm your dad - dy, I'm that nig -

ger in the al - ley. I'm your doc - tor when in need, _ want some coke, have some weed. You know me,

I'm your friend, your main boy, thick and thin. I'm your push-er man.

I'm your push-er man.

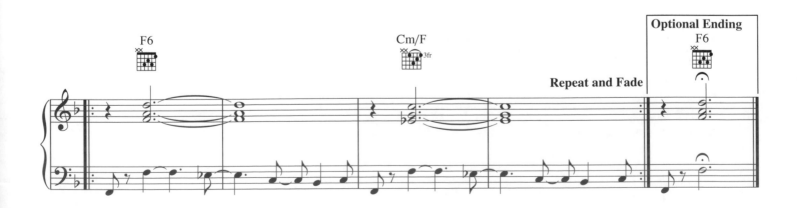

Repeat and Fade

Optional Ending